Science Matters
PRECIPITATION

Frances Purslow

WEIGL PUBLISHERS INC.

Published by Weigl Publishers Inc.
350 5th Avenue, Suite 3304, PMB 6G
New York, NY USA 10118-0069
Web site: www.weigl.com
Copyright 2006 WEIGL PUBLISHERS INC.

*J
551.57
Pur*

Library of Congress Cataloging-in-Publication Data

Purslow, Frances.
  Precipitation / Frances Purslow.
      p. cm. -- (Science matters)
  Includes index.
  ISBN 1-59036-305-1 (alk. paper) -- ISBN 1-59036-311-6 (pbk. : alk. paper)
  1. Precipitation (Meteorology)--Juvenile literature. I. Title. II. Series.
  QC920.P87 2005
  551.57'7--dc22

                              2004028942

Printed in the United States of America
1 2 3 4 5 6 7 8 9 0 09 08 07 06 05

Project Coordinator Tina Schwartzenberger
Copy Editor Heather C. Hudak
Design Terry Paulhus **Layout** Kathryn Livingstone
Photo Researcher Jason Novak

17.10

Contents

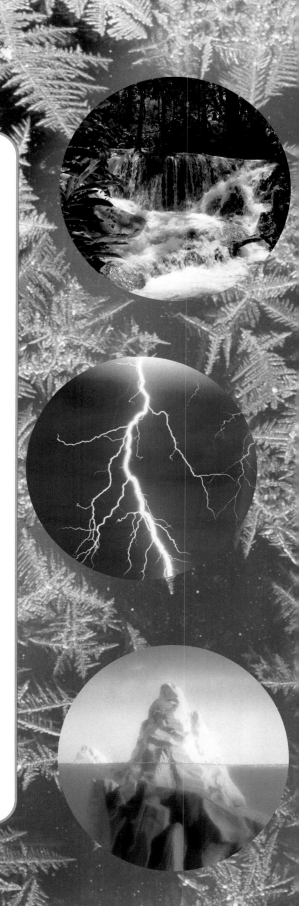

Studying Precipitation

The atmosphere is a blanket of gases that surrounds Earth. One of the gases in the atmosphere is **water vapor**. It rises from oceans, lakes, and other bodies of water when the Sun warms them. Water vapor cools as it rises. Then, it **condenses** and forms tiny drops of water. When the drops become large enough, they fall as rain or snow. Water that falls to Earth in solid or liquid form is called precipitation.

■ Earth's atmosphere is divided into layers. Most clouds form in the lowest layer, closest to Earth.

Precipitation Facts

Did you know that 4 trillion gallons (15 trillion liters) of precipitation fall on the United States every day? Here are more interesting facts about precipitation.

- Ten inches (30 centimeters) of snow contain as much water as 1 inch (2 cm) of rain.

- Cherrapunji, India, holds the record for the most rainfall in 1 year—more than 80 feet (24 meters).

- At all times, the atmosphere contains enough water for 1 inch (2.5 cm) of rain to fall on Earth.

- Earth is not the only planet where frost forms. Frost sometimes covers the ground on Mars, too.

- Very little precipitation falls at the North Pole. The snow that falls at the North Pole does not melt.

Types of Precipitation

There are many types of precipitation. Rain falls when the weather is warm. Rain becomes snow when the weather is cold.

A   *dew*: water vapor that condenses on plants after a cool night

B   *frost*: frozen water vapor or dew that forms when condensation freezes

C   *sleet*: melting snow or freezing rain

D   *hail*: balls of ice that form when the temperature is just below freezing

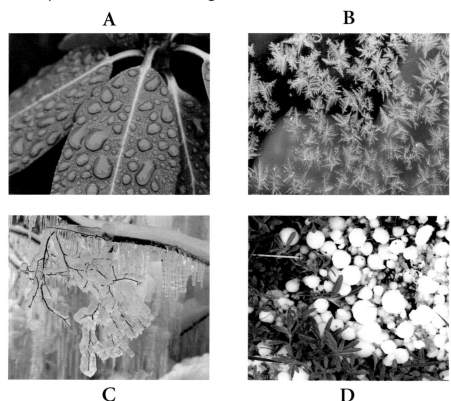

A

B

C

D

Six-sided Wonders

When cooled, water vapor condenses into water drops. In temperatures below freezing, these water drops become snowflakes. Each snowflake is made from tiny pieces of ice that stick together.

All snowflakes have six sides. Although snowflakes may look the same, no two snowflakes are alike. Each has a different pattern of frozen water **molecules**.

- An average snowflake falls at a speed of 3 miles (5 kilometers) per hour.

Water Vapor

Clouds and fog are water vapor. Clouds form when water vapor condenses around tiny pieces of dust. Fog is a thick mist of water vapor in the air, near the ground. Sometimes, water droplets join together to form larger drops of water. These drops of water fall to the ground as precipitation.

■ Falling raindrops are shaped like hamburger patties. They are squashed balls with flat tops and bottoms.

Rain Folklore

Some people believe that stepping on a spider causes rain. For many years, people have tried to predict the weather by watching how animals act.

Here are some other signs that people believed were a sign of rain.

- bees returning to their hives

- ants building barriers around their nests

- cattle lying down in the field

- flies collecting on window and door screens

- butterflies flying from the southwest

- cats washing their ears

Storms

Storms have strong winds and precipitation. A blizzard is a bad winter storm that can last for many hours. During a blizzard, strong winds blow large amounts of snow through the air.

Freezing rain falls during an ice storm. The air is usually warm enough for rain, but the ground is very cold. Streets and sidewalks become very slippery. Tree branches and power lines break under the weight of the heavy ice.

A storm with thunder, lightning, and heavy rain is a thunderstorm. Clouds contain electricity. When electricity moves between clouds or between a cloud and the ground, we see a flash of light. This flash is lightning. The loud rumbling or cracking sound that follows lightning is thunder.

● The average lightning strike is 6 miles (10 km) long.

Cloud Seeding

Scientists can use technology to create storms or make them less severe. They add chemicals to clouds to change them. This is called cloud seeding.

Clouds are seeded for many reasons:

- Fog over airports is seeded to reduce the cloud's density, or thickness. Planes can land and take off safely when the fog is less dense.

- Cloud seeding can prevent lightning. This reduces the number of forest fires started by lightning.

- Cloud seeding can produce 12 to 14 percent more rain in dry areas where rain is needed.

- Cloud seeding softens hail. Softer hail causes less damage to crops, homes, and businesses.

The Water Cycle

Earth has a limited amount of water. Water **recycles** itself through the water cycle. This diagram shows how the water cycle works.

Precipitation

Glaciers

Lakes

Trees

Floods

Rain and snow do not fall evenly across Earth. Some places receive much more precipitation than others. Rivers flood when too much water flows into them. If too much rain falls or too much snow and ice melt quickly, rivers may **overflow**.

Some countries have a monsoon **climate**. Monsoons are very strong winds. During the summer, the wind blows from the sea toward land. Large amounts of rain usually fall during summer monsoons. In the winter, the wind blows from land toward the sea.

■ Summer monsoons bring large amounts of rain and can cause floods. Winter monsoons bring very little moisture.

Drought

A long period of dry weather is called a drought. Animals and plants may die from the lack of water. Drought can also cause bushfires and dust storms.

In the 1930s, about 75 percent of the United States had a drought. Crops died, and huge dust storms swept across many states. Texas, Oklahoma, Kansas, Colorado, and New Mexico became known as the "Dust Bowl" because they were so dry.

On April 14, 1935, millions of tons of **topsoil** blew across the plains. This day was called "Black Sunday" because of the huge cloud of thick, black dust.

Weather Forecasting

Meteorologists are people who predict the weather. They predict how much precipitation will fall in certain areas. Meteorologists use computer models of the atmosphere to predict weather. They look for clouds on photographs taken by satellites, which are a type of spacecraft. Meteorologists also locate clouds using **radar**.

■ Meteorologists use computers to track large storms such as hurricanes.

What Causes a Rainbow?

Sometimes a rainbow appears in the sky during or after rain. The Sun and raindrops work together to make a rainbow.

Although light looks white, it is actually a mix of many colors. These colors mix together, so people cannot see them. A raindrop refracts, or bends, light so that a band of colors, or a rainbow, appears. The rainbow's colors are red, orange, yellow, green, blue, indigo, and violet.

Acid Rain

Air **pollution** has been a growing problem over the past few hundred years. It is caused by smoke and chemicals from factories and vehicles. When rain falls through air pollution, the water mixes with the pollution. The water becomes **acid rain**. Acid rain kills trees, crops, and lakes. Over time, it can even damage stone.

Acid rain has damaged more than 60 percent of the forests in the Czech Republic.

Acid Rain Experiment

You can create the effects of acid rain in your kitchen. Chalk is limestone, a soft form of marble. Vinegar is a mild acid. See what happens when they mix together.

You will need:

- a glass
- vinegar
- a small piece of white blackboard chalk

Place the chalk at the bottom of the glass. Pour enough vinegar into the glass to completely cover the chalk. The next day, look at the chalk. Has it changed?

Over long periods of time, acid rain can even damage marble. Many of the world's great marble statues and buildings are in danger of damage from acid rain.

Surfing Water Science

How can I find more information about precipitation?

- Libraries have many interesting books about precipitation.
- Science centers and museums are great places to learn more about precipitation.
- The Internet offers some great Web sites dedicated to precipitation.

Where can I find a good reference Web site to learn more about precipitation?

Encarta Homepage
www.encarta.com

- Type any precipitation-related term into the search engine. Some terms to try include "snow" and "acid rain."

How can I find out more about precipitation and the water cycle?

Wild Wild Weather
www.wildwildweather.com/precipitation.htm

- This Web site was created for kids by a meteorologist. It has games, puzzles, and experiments.

Science in Action

Build a Rain Gauge

Weather forecasters measure rainfall using a rain gauge. A rain gauge collects rain and measures the depth of the water.

You will need:

- scissors
- a large empty plastic soda bottle
- marbles or stones
- masking tape
- a ruler
- a marker
- water

Ask an adult to cut the top off the soda bottle. Put a handful of stones or marbles in the bottom of the bottle to help the bottle stay upright. Cut a strip of masking tape 4 inches (10 cm) long.

Place the strip of tape lengthwise on the side of the bottle above the level of the stones. Use the ruler and marker to draw lines on the tape. The lines should be 0.25 inches (0.6 cm) apart.

Pour water into the bottle until it reaches the bottom of the tape. This is where you will begin your measurements. Now, put your rain gauge outside to collect rain. Your rain gauge will also measure snowfall.

What Have You Learned?

1. How much water is in 12 inches (30 cm) of snow?

2. What causes a rainbow?

3. Name three types of precipitation.

4. What are the seven colors of a rainbow?

5. What shape is a raindrop?

6 How many sides does a snowflake have?

7 What is a person who predicts the weather called?

8 Why are clouds seeded?

9 How much of the United States experienced drought in the 1930s?

10 What is acid rain?

Answers: 1. 1 inch (2.5 cm) **2.** Sunlight shining through raindrops **3.** Rain, snow, sleet, hail, dew, or frost **4.** Red, orange, yellow, green, blue, indigo, and violet **5.** Raindrops are shaped like hamburger patties or squashed balls with flat tops and bottoms. **6.** Six **7.** A meteorologist **8.** To produce rain for dry areas, to soften hail, to reduce fog density, and to prevent lightning **9.** 75 percent **10.** Rain mixed with air pollution

Words to Know

acid rain: rain mixed with air pollution that damages plants, water, and the environment

climate: the usual weather in a region throughout the year

condenses: changes from gas to liquid

molecules: the smallest pieces that a substance can be divided into without changing it into another substance

overflow: to flow over the surface or limits of an area

pollution: harmful materials, such as gases, chemicals, and waste, that dirty air, water, and soil

radar: a system that uses radio waves to locate objects

recycles: returns to an original condition so a process can begin again

topsoil: the upper layer of soil

water vapor: water in the form of a gas

Index